Wife-Mom-Preneur

My Journey

First Edition: December 2018

Author's Note: *This work is a memoir. Events,
actions and their consequences over a period of
time have been retold as the author presently
remembers them. Some names and identifying
details have been changed to protect the privacy
of those involved, and some dialogue has been
re-created from memory.*

Library of Congress Cataloging-in-Publications
Data

Tramika Craddock

Wife-Mom-Preneur. My Journey

ISBN: 978-0-578-42105-6

To every Wife, Mother, Entrepreneur… Woman…

Who has ever felt lost and didn't understand their purpose…

To every Wife, Mother, Entrepreneur… Woman…

Who has every become over-whelmed, frustrated, tired, fatigue, stressed and have even sometimes felt as if you couldn't or didn't know how you would put the next foot forward because of the weight of responsibilities…

To every Wife, Mother, Entrepreneur… Woman…

Who all you know is, you just want to be your very best in every area of your life…

This book is for YOU!

CONTENT

PREFACE

As women we often get lost in the shadows of other responsibilities such as being a wife or a mother, or employee. The juggling act of being, *"Terrell's Wife, His Wife," "Samai, Terrell & Kaniya's Mom"* or *"Employee of the Month,"* are labels that have been added to the HATS I wear. While these HATS are honorable and worth wearing, I sometimes question my purpose. *What about my own identity? What about my talents and gifts that I know I can use to change the world?*

In 2009 I was laid off from what I considered, the Best job I ever had! This was my dream job. The money, the people, even the company culture was everything I wanted. This was my ticket to success. The day I received the phone call not to return to work was a crippling blow - that security was immediately snatched as if someone had ripped my stomach right out of my body. Taking this away not only destroyed my dream of climbing the corporate ladder, but also would have an immediate impact on my family. *How would we pay all our bills? How would we take care of our children?* For so long, I rested my security in a job. Not in my spouse or in God as I should have. Laid off from what I considered to be the perfect job and my pathway to success in life. *What was I to do now?* After much discussion with my Husband, I decided not to hurry back into corporate America but to take some time and go back to school full-time. A few classes a week meant lots of free time at home, I was now a "House-Wife!" and *I was loving it!!!* My purpose would be taking care of my husband and my children, day in and day out, meeting all their needs and helping them in any way possible. After just a few short months, I found myself settling in the role of *"The House Wife."* Life was great! Life was great for my home, my family, and me. I have found a rhythm that worked for my family and our home… The only thing was that rhythm did not include me.

As I settled into the role of being a great House Wife, the newness of being called, *"Terrell's wife, His wife, Kaniya's Mom, Samai's Mom"* began to wear off. I began asking myself the question, *"what about me?"* More and more my answer to people would be, *"I have a name too!"* I wanted my identity to be known, for all my hard work and efforts as a House-Wife.

I noticed that not only was I not getting any recognition for being the House-Wife, I became comfortable not going anywhere, not purchasing things for myself, not caring for me as much as I cared for my family.

NOW! Don't get me wrong, I'm ALWAYS here to support and push my husband and my kids*, but what about my own dreams and desires for my life???* Should I just forget about them because I'm now a house-wife, *is this my future?*

My answer was to jump back into Corporate America. Back to the hustle and bustle of office life! Highway traffic, packed parking lots, busy revolving doors, packed elevators, the smell of coffee as you exited the elevator on your work floor, the innocent and not so innocent good mornings as you made your way to your desk, the 100 million emails that waited for you to be read by the time you clocked in to take the first call. It felt good to be back, it felt good to know as soon as I entered the building I was going to make a difference in someone's life, that my "Boss" would be proud of me and want me to train others to be just as great as I was. Even after my move back to Corporate America, there was still something missing! That tug to follow my dreams kept stirring in the pit of my stomach. My dreams were starving; trying to claw their way out of this dying Woman. I ignored it and nestled into of the comfort of working for someone else. I felt like a mother refusing to give birth; lying there with my legs crossed, refusing to push! I hid behind *"The House-wife, the Loving Wife, The Loving Mother, the Full-Time Employee."* The pain was becoming unbearable. This baby was coming, whether I was ready or not! It was finally time to start becoming who I was called to be. Yes, I needed to be a loving wife to my husband. Yes, I needed to be a loving mother to my children. But, I also needed to say YES to Tramika! I had finally made the decision to do ALL those things AND follow My Dreams!

Was my transformation difficult at times? Absolutely! I still have difficult days! My success is finding the right balance, methods, plans, strategies that would work for me and my family. Life can get busy and with a husband and 3 kids, I'm always busy! But I had to find a way to not be too busy for Tramika! I had to find a way to be a wife, mother and still go after my dreams. It took a lot of planning, a lot of tweaking, lots of failure and lots of me not giving up! One of the BEST parts of my story is the part where *I didn't give up!*

WIFE

Wife-*A female partner in Marriage*

Merriam-Webster definition

Wife-*A woman who marries the love of her life, who becomes overwhelmed in happiness and who is unconditionally loved by her spouse. Her husband adores everything about her and seeks to please her any way possible and takes care of her until the day she dies-*

Tramika's definition

But, here's what really happened…

The Day Everything Will Change

August 19th, 2006! In North Carolina. The day I get to marry my High School Sweetheart!

I couldn't believe I came home last night and slept in the same bed as Terrell, the night before the wedding. It's tradition; the groom is not supposed to see the bride on the day of the wedding-before she walked down the aisle. Oh well, I told myself. A lot of things in our relationship had been untraditional, *a lot!* Especially the fact that we were already parents. We also married young, just 21 and 22. I was wearing my mom's dress for this special occasion. That's enough tradition, I chuckled to myself. Everything was causing frustration trying to plan and get this wedding executed in such a short period of time, and I couldn't imagine myself anywhere else but in the comfort of my own home and my warm bed to ease my frustration and help me relax, the night before my wedding. If my frustration turned into a bad attitude, that was going to be a problem for everyone! I laid there and continued to think about my day. Everything was happening so fast! I moved to North Carolina in April of that year and decided to plan a wedding for August. *Four months, who does that?* Planning this was so hard. My only options for bridal stores, rental halls, churches, etc. were limited, in this new town I now called home. Terrell was already here for a while and I had moved here with the intentions of us marrying but it all happened so fast, before I could even settle in. To tell you the truth, I'm not sure how much Terrell knew about the town either. I decided to follow him here and marry him. *Wait, was I being a fool?* I followed him here…*Nah, I love him, I'm in love with him…right?* Still laying in the bed, all these thoughts started to cross my mind. We had been through so much as just teenagers. *Was I making a mistake?* I had missed my Best Friend's wedding because of our wedding date, the second opportunity to be a bridesmaid had passed me. I had already missed being in my mother's wedding because I was very pregnant with our first child. Missing my Best Friend's wedding was a hard pill to swallow though. *Would she ever even forgive me?* I justified it all... Terrell and I wanted our parents at our wedding, but they lived in New York. The wedding date we chose was convenient for them and happened to be the weekend right after my Best Friend's wedding. I was sad, but I could not miss an opportunity for my family to be back together. An opportunity for my daughter to have her father in the home with her. An opportunity I thought I would never have. See we had broken up 6 months after our first daughter was born but eventually we both got saved and decided to make things work for our family. *Sad or glad, I was marrying this man and I was going to do it on any day I could!* I wanted a small wedding. I knew it would not be as lavish as I had always imagined. Four months was not a lot of time to pull off a lavish wedding. With our parents and siblings, we would have just enough people to bear witness, that's all we needed. *Then we would live happily ever after… right?* Isn't that how it worked? That ending was in every book I read, every television show and movie I watched. I convinced myself that yes, my life would be the same. The small wedding that I had imagined grew quickly into something much bigger. Our new church family in North Carolina would attend, as well as a host of Terrell's family members who would travel from New York. What was supposed to be no more than 9 guests was now almost 50.

Around 7am on the morning of my big day, I got out of the bed and looked at my phone. I had almost 10 missed calls from Sister Kay. She was a kind church member who had invited me to stay with her the night before my wedding. Sister Kay would accompany me with two other women, to the hair salon and to get my makeup done. You know, all the pampering a bride gets on her big day. I could only imagine how worried she was. I didn't even bother to call her. With a long sigh and a couple of deep breaths, I cleared my mind, so I could get my day started.

"Do you feel nervous?" Everyone keeps asking me that, rolling my eyes. No, I wasn't. I had known this man since 2001. We had partially lived together. *Wait, is partially even possible?* We *LIVED* together! We have a daughter together, we had been through so much together, good and bad, I thought as a huge smile spread across my face. Suddenly, I went into a small panic as I thought about the bad more than the good. *Was I making the right decision? Was I a fool for marrying this man?* Nope, No fool here! I love this man. Today will be the day that everything is going to change. It will be like magic and our past wrong-doings, our past hurts, all that negative junk, will *POOF*, just like magic, be gone! Today is a new day! A new beginning! I know what God told me about my man. But who was I trying to convince, everyone else or *me*?

Hair done, makeup done. Not by MAC
Cosmetics I thought, frowning with a huge
attitude, I remember just thinking how much I
didn't like my makeup on one of the most
important days of my life, but I guess it would do.
Wait, I reallyyy don't like it! Ugh! Maybe the veil
will cover all the flaws. I didn't have a choice at
this point. My next thought was praying I would
fit into this dress. I was honored to be wearing
my mom's dress. Shoot! Who was I fooling? I
was saving a lot of money! I wondered if my
daughter would wear it. We could start a family
tradition. Once I arrived at the church I started to
ask myself, *"Are you nervous yet? Will you get
nervous? Is THIS what nervousness feels like?"*
Nah, this should be a piece of cake! We have
only known each other since forever. Looking
around the church I saw people buzzing, running
from one place to another; making sure
everything was just right. I thought to myself, it's
pretty, but we better not start late! I thought
about how cold the church was, I mean it was
freezing. I found my way to the room that was

set up just for me, the bride, it was my own little sanctuary, so I could get ready.

I was dressed and waiting with a coat on. It seemed as if every 5 minutes someone would peek in the room to check on me. I started to get confused. What the heck was going on? Why was everyone coming in here and why weren't they calling me out? Had the service even started yet??! Man, it's about to start late and I felt it was getting late and all the while I could feel a bad attitude rising out of me like a pot of boiling water. I heard the whispers in the hallway. Something was wrong, I just knew it! *Did he change his mind?* Was some part of the decorations left behind? Did no one show up? After sitting there for what seemed liked hours, that feeling became a reality. Terrell was late because he got a flat tire. Wait, what? What did he drive over, a nail? Why didn't he go around it? *It's our wedding day!* Did he hit a curb? Why did he drive so close? *It's our wedding day!* Was he driving too fast, if so why didn't he slow down? *It's our wedding day!* And just like that pot of boiling water that begins to rise and spill over if you don't move it fast enough from the eye on the stove, I was ready to boil over too. I hated to be late. I still wasn't nervous, just ready to get things over with. But all I could do was wait.

After what seemed like forever I was upstairs in the foyer outside the sanctuary. The doors to the sanctuary were closed in front of me, butterflies began to build in my stomach. This was it. The day, the moment that everything would change. I am marrying the man that I am so deeply in love with. My family would now be complete. How blessed was I that God put my family back together again. How blessed was I that I would marry my high school sweetheart. How blessed, even after everything we went through, as teenagers and even as young adults, figuring out our feelings and trying to grow up, but grow together at the same time, we made it! A few minutes more and we would be standing before God, family, and lots of witnesses to say, *"I do."*

We would live happily ever after. We could finally have sex without feeling guilty. And I do mean a LOT of sex. Any time; just good 'ole Godly, legal sex that would be gracious in God's eyes! My days of repenting were over.

What led to this day wasn't exactly what I had read in books. Not quite how it played out on the television shows and in movies. One thing I was sure of, this was THE day; the moment that everything would change for the both of us. The doors opened to the sanctuary and it was finally time for me to walk in. With every step I made, those butterflies in my stomach seemed to grow bigger and multiply all at the same time; the feeling was out of control. I decided my way to fight this feeling was through laughing. If my guests laughed, then I would too. If I saw any tears, I would just ignore them. Bet, that would work, I convinced myself! I made a funny face as I took my next step. Then, I started laughing to ease my nerves. Soon those butterflies that were growing in my stomach suddenly became the wings beneath my feet that carried me to the finish line. I felt like I had just floated all the way down the aisle to the altar.

That walk down the aisle was way too fast! My brain couldn't catch up with everything I did and everyone I saw. There were a lot of faces, but to this day couldn't tell you who they were; everything was just so blurry.! I saw my Pastor straight ahead, standing in black and white and had a few glimpses at Terrell. I even think he cried, how sweet! Standing at the altar going through the ceremony, going through the motions, repeating everything she says going through the rituals designed in the ceremony. I was so nervous! I wanted to scream, *"Stop looking at me!"* They were watching every sneeze, every cough; just EVERYTHING! I thought to myself, *Oh my God! Am I really marrying this man?* He is Kaniya's Father, but what about this… and what about that? Tramika are you really doing THIS at this altar? I remember that I was so in love with him when we first met. We came into each other's lives when a serious void needed to be filled. We were there for each other like no one else could be. Our bond grew, and it grew fast. But what about all the pain and hurt I endured during the time we had broken up after having our first daughter? Lord, that pain is still here! *"Pain"* was smiling and standing at this altar, dressed up in a suit, ready to enter the marriage with us. I could slap that grin right off his face. Better yet, why is he, "pain," here with us Lord! That pain just sucker punched me in my stomach, without anyone even seeing it. Now standing up straight right between us, waiting to enter the marriage as if its name was on the marriage license too. As if it was waiting on the Pastor to say, *"I now pronounce you Husband, Wife and Pain."* Yep, the pain was bold and was not about to back down. Why is this happening? God, when Terrell told me I was his wife, I prayed I asked you! You confirmed a yes in my spirit! As quickly as those thoughts entered my mind, God whispered to me, *"Let it go."* The sanctuary got brighter, the smiles from the audience were bigger; I didn't see the Pain, well-dressed and standing at the altar, any longer. He probably knew I was about to slap the crap out of him for ruining my day; taking away from my moment... Oh God, after all we been through. I never thought you would give me an opportunity to have my family together. *Do I even deserve this?* God, I thank you! *"Hallelujah"* I hadn't even realized I said it out loud, I just hoped it was befitting with where we were in the ceremony. I didn't care if anyone heard me. All I knew was that one word was a release. Then started the praise. *"Thank you, Jesus." "Thank you, God."* All at the altar while the tears flowed. When I came to myself, I realized that I was not the only one praising God at this moment, Terrell, my soon to be Husband, was also praising God and our Pastor was about to preach! Looking back, that praise session we had was not only the most hilarious thing, but also the most important thing. Little did I know at that moment, that the church we had at the altar would soon keep our marriage together.

Finally, *"I DO"* Now what? It doesn't feel any different. Well, at least I'm no longer nervous. I'm no longer crying. I didn't expect rainbows or some melody from heaven, but I thought to myself, *shouldn't there be more?* Like, instantly be more? After all, this is the day that would change everything… *right?* A new beginning, the past is erased… *right?*

"D" is for Divorce; or is it?

Well, well, well! Someone lied about the happily ever after! I was mad, disappointed; the worst attitude to make this marriage work. Let me be clear, we had some good days, but no one ever told us about the days that would be *HELL.* I loved my Man! I didn't see any ideal marriages around me, So I was determined that our marriage would be everything that those marriages weren't! I was going to do my best to copy what I had read in books. I was going to do what I had seen in the movies! Dancing for him, dressing up for him, cooking for him, rubbing his head, enticing him, flirting with him-all that and more. The day after we came home as husband and wife, I put a chair in our room, turned Destiny's Child's *"Cater to You."* While the words to that song played in the background, I was ready! I had even repeated those words to myself, trying to keep my mind in the right place.

This is exactly how I'm going to be to my Man! Yes, my Man! I had a husband and I was ready to fulfill his every need! Or so I thought! *Chile, that lasted for like 3 days!* Why didn't anyone tell me I was in a fantasy world? Why didn't they tell me that I was not going to be able to be the person I wanted to be without any compromise; love this man and he was going to love me back! Every part of me-the good, the bad and the ugly. I can't even remember what our first disagreement was. What I do know was that it happened less than a week after we were married. I remember our wedding pictures and some of his clothes thrown across the front lawn. You can guess who threw what out there. I just want to get to the bottom of who lied to me about this marriage thing! I felt like going back to every author of the fairy tale books all those writers of every television show and movie I had seen, and yell, *"Ya'll are ALL liars!"* How dare you set me up to believe the hype: this beautiful picture of marital bliss and happiness, a big house on the hill with a white picket fence, dogs running around the yard, women dressing up in pumps and having a million outfits to change into, and wives helping their husbands pick out the best tie for his suit; all a bunch of lies thought up by a bunch of liars! The lie played out in my head, in living color and theater surround sound.

The husband and wife, both with great careers, kiss each other lovingly each morning before leaving home. They drop their well-behaved kids off at school. At the end of the day, both come home and are greeted by the family dog wagging his tail to show his eagerness to see them. After the wife starts dinner, she helps the kids with their homework. Suddenly, she feels her husband's hands slip around her waist. Their passions rise as he leads her to their bedroom. They make passionate love and return to children playing with the dog, pots simmering-everything just as perfect as they left it.

LIES, LIES, LIES!!! Sometimes you don't have great careers, sometimes you don't feel like looking at your spouse, yet alone kissing them, the kids are definitely not always well-behaved, sometimes you don't feel like helping the kids with homework, sometimes your husband comes home stressed because he hates his job and has the weight of the world on his shoulders and he walks pass you cooking and goes to take a nap and tells you to wake him when the food is done, and sometimes those kids who not so well behaved will get into everything while you try to go sneak away for some passionate love, sometimes even the family dog not happy! *LIES!* I was lied to growing up! I felt deceived! You see, our house was full of attitude; plenty of neck rolling, eyes rolling, attitudes, facing the window silently as we drove home, rolling over so far to the outside of the bed that we almost fell out. Don't get me wrong we had some good days. We laughed, we joked, we ate together, watched shows together, of course the legal sex was always good but it wasn't a lot of those days any more. As a matter fact there weren't enough of them at all! It made me question this marriage early on; *did I make a mistake?* This is sure not what I signed up for! This is not what I imagined, and I refuse to spend the rest of my life like this! Early in our marriage after a very heated argument, we both decided that enough was enough. I thought to myself, this is not what I signed up for; this is not what the marriage looked like that I read about in books; this was not the fairy tale ending that I always thought I would have! I was done. I tried. It was over. Like idiots, (*yes, I said like idiots*) we drove to the courthouse together to file for a divorce. He was looking straight ahead during the ride and I was screw-faced, mad, looking out the window. Sitting so close to the window that if would have fallen right out if anyone was to open the door. I was upset, and I was done! We loved each other, but we came from two different worlds. Our likes and dislikes were different, we didn't share many things in common. Most of all we were young, still trying to figure out who we were, yet alone trying to make the proper adjustments and sacrifices to please each other. Despite the big argument, we loved each other so much that we decided to call it quits before things would get any worse. Let's just be *"friends!"* It was a long drive to the courthouse that day, probably the longest ride ever or at least it felt like it! I sat there in the passenger seat like a bump on the log, my elbow leaning on the door, my hand under my chin, looking out the window, wondering how I got here and how I just wanted to have peace in my life. See I had gone through so much in my past, my childhood, I was determined to be loved and be in peace in my life, the true meaning to that was being spoiled and having everything my way because I was dealt wrong by some many other people in my life. But that's not how marriage worked! I know that now, but on this day... We seemed to jump out of the car in our misguided eagerness. We entered the building, went through the metal detectors, and rode on the elevator to the Clerk's office. We approached the counter when it was our turn. The woman at the counter said, "How can I help you?" My reply was both quick and stern. "We are here to file for a divorce!" She had a blank stare on her face and went back and forth looking at the both of us. My soon to be ex-husband *(or so I thought)* stood there so firm in his demeanor as if he was saying, "that's right," without uttering a word. I know she had to be completely baffled. *What couple comes together to file for a divorce?* I was sure she was either laughing on the inside or thought we were complete idiots. Who knows, she might have thought, poor kids. The woman at the counter asked us if we were married in the state of North Carolina, we nodded and said, "Yes." She then proceeded to ask how long we had been separated. My husband and I both looking confused and frustrated at this point, thinking why does THAT even matter. We told her two days. Two days, where he slept on the couch and I slept in the bed. *That's separated, right??* We had decided to end it all. Although we were still under the same roof, in our minds we were very much apart. There was that awkward silence again, the woman at the counter probably cracked up laughing all over again in the inside. She then proceeded to tell us that in the state of North Carolina, you had to be separated at least ONE year before you can file for a divorce. My heart dropped in disbelief. The look on my face was probably worth a million dollars of at least a good Meme. My husband and I both stood there stunned and after staring back at her in silence for about 15 seconds, turned around and walked out, it was a long quiet walk down the hallway, long quiet ride back down the elevator, out the double doors, to the car and a long ride home. *What were we going to do?* There was no way we could be separated for a year. First of all, we couldn't afford it! We had to stay under the same roof, well whatever, let the year of separation begin! Barely speaking and playing with our daughter louder than ever so the other person could hear, we tried our best to be *"separated"* so that we could get through the year and properly file for a divorce. After a few days our physical needs always got the best of us! There was no way! It was something about making up after a blow up, I mean it was just

DIFFERENT! After years of throwing around the "D" word. I mean "divorce," not the other "D" word (*you are so nasty!*) We reached the conclusion that neither one of us was going anywhere. By then we had our second child had been born and we were in too deep to walk away. It was like every time we decided we wanted to be mad at each other something would happen where we would have to talk. One time I got a flat tire at work and had to call him, another time our daughter had to go to the doctors suddenly, so we had to talk, it was something that just drew us back together each time. At this point in my life I realized that I was in this for life, *"until death do us 'part!"* I felt lost though.; as I had no great examples of marriages or wives around me. *How was I going to be a wife to this man when I had never seen how it was done the right way? How would I fulfil his needs when I had so many wounds from my past and needs of my own? How was I going to love this man properly and I was abandoned by the first man in my life, my father? Who was I to call? Who was I to get help from? What was I supposed to do? What is a wife technically? And what role does she play in the marriage?* These were all the questions I asked myself. I didn't know where to start, but I knew I loved my husband. I didn't want a broken home for my family. I knew that anything I was determined to get in life, I got it. It was going to be challenging but I was up for the challenge. Although all of this happened in the very beginning of our marriage, we threw the *"D"* word around more after this, it was an instant change. Patterns and behaviors had to change. The journey was long, it was frustrating, and it was hurtful. All while trying to please this man, my husband I had to deal with my own open wounds, it was painful! It wasn't until about our 8th year of marriage that we really decided that the *"D" word (divorce)* was no longer acceptable in our marriage, that we were playing for keeps and we realized that we would conquer whatever comes our way, TOGETHER!

I then became determined more than ever that I would not be a reflection to all the broken marriages that I had seen growing up. I was determined more than ever to not be a single, divorced woman raising kids alone. I was determined more than ever to not allow my children to have step-parents! I was determined to fight the fight and keep my Man! But I not only wanted a Marriage that would survive, I wanted a marriage that would thrive. I wanted to be loved the way I needed to be loved, I wanted to meet his needs as his wife. After much prayer, more prayer, research, making mistakes, learning from mistakes, good counsel and more prayer I'm happy to say that I am that loving wife that I didn't know how to be in the beginning of our marriage. I know my husband and his ways, and I know how to fulfil his needs and take care of him as his wife. I am now living the life I desired as a wife. My life is better than the stories I read because it is real, and it is authentic. Most of all our marriage testimony helps other couples move to that place of success faster than we did. We learned and experienced a lot on our own but that made us wise! Our marriage is not perfect and I'm NOT a Perfect Wife, but we are perfectly imperfect together. I am *(and still becoming)* the Wife that God has called me to be. One thing is for sure, the "D" word is no longer allowed in my marriage. Divorce is no longer an option. From the beginning, I was determined to win! I was determined to win for my children who deserved both parents in the household and for my children who would grow up, knowing what marriage was because they had seen it first hand from their parents. I was determined to win for all the people who were watching who we encouraged and inspired and the people who was watching who found strength from what appeared to be our strength! I was determined to win for the man that I had married when I stood before God and witnesses and told him I Do, for better or for worse! I always knew even when we were dating that I was the balance he needed in life and that he was my balance, besides everyone else, we owed it to ourselves to try and not give up on US! I was determined for myself, to give love a try, I have been hurt by so many people and for so many years of my life. There were moments when I was hurt in this relationship but there were more moments where I was loved, where I was understood, when I was spoiled, when I was adored, when I was respected and when I was valued. If every day could just be like that but I knew that wasn't realistic… God if most days could be like that I would be happy. And out of all those people the most important reason why I was determined is because I owed it to God. After all I did make a vow before Him. In that moment, that short moment that I was spiritual I came to the conclusion that I owed God because of the vows I made. I took that thought and ran with it! Before I became carnal again; before reality set in and he got on my nerves again… Yes, I was determined to ride this thing called marriage until the wheels fell off!

From that point on I was determined to be the best wife that I could be. Yes, I still make mistakes, yes sometimes I fall short. It is not easy! DAILY, when I say daily, I literally mean that, more like hourly for me at first, I had to die to my flesh, cast down negative thoughts of the past and dwell on our future together. Before I was married, I was a mom. Seems backwards, right? Well that's my story! So, for me it was how do I fit marriage in to parenting when really it should have been the other way. The covenant of marriage had to come first. I learned daily how to become a better wife. I also realized that my "becoming" was not easy, nor was it an immediate change for me. Yes, I still hear things like, *"Can you pencil me in?"* and *"I wish you would do that for me like you do it for them kids."* It's so easy to set aside the needs of your spouse because you are human number one, but because they are an adult. Have you ever felt like *"can't you do it"* or *"can't you get it"* or *"I'm tired right now, later?"* These are normal feelings when you are trying to balance marriage, children... balance life! It doesn't mean that you are a bad wife. It's important that we re-adjust our levels to make sure every area is getting its proper amount of YOU!

Over the years for some reason everyone looked at our Marriage and thought it was always perfect. I remember telling someone randomly one day that Terrell and I weren't talking to each other. Their response was *"What?! Y'all don't look like y'all ever disagree!"* That comment was the funniest thing ever! We were far from perfect. See my journey to becoming the wife I desired to wasn't easy because I was in a perfect marriage. It was difficult because we were two different people with different upbringings, attempting to become one. I had to make the decision to be the best person I could be in our Marriage. It wasn't on anyone else but me.

MOM

Mom noun: (mäm)

Short for Mother.

A person's mother.

Merriam-Webster definition

(n)-A woman who raises her kids to be the best they can be. Perfect in the eyes of her children. "My Mom is the best."

(adj)-Nurturing; vigilant in her duties to her kids. "She was in Mom mode."

(v)-Protecting her kids at every waking moment. "I heard my baby's cry; I mom(ed) up."

Tramika's definition

But, again here's what really happened…

How did I get here?

Three little people who were my total responsibility! Even though I was more confident about being a Mother than a Wife I really didn't know what I was doing. I was more confident being a mom because I knew that I could raise them and mode them into someone who would be special to the world. See for me, marriage was much more different. You entered a relationship with someone who had a mind and plans of their own. Children weren't like that, they don't know any better and they depend and rely on you, as the parent, to show them the way. I didn't know how to exactly be a "mom," I just knew that I wanted their lives to be so different from mine and that I wanted them to experience better than I did and be better as a child and as they grew up. I could remember there were so many times as a child I felt lonely and sad. I didn't want this for my children. The determination was kind of there from the beginning. I just didn't know what the end goal looked like and the proper steps to get there. I just knew from the beginning what I didn't want it to look like! Being a mother does not come with a manual unfortunately; *how cool would that be?*

At this age add a pinch of reading, a teaspoon of spankings and a cup of Jesus. Do this every week for 2 years and you will have the perfect toddler by the time they are 3 they will be *"perfect"* children.

So, I made my own recipe: A hint of instinct; add a pinch of reading, a teaspoon of spankings, and a big ol' cup of Jesus; repeat every week (well, at least for the first 2 years) and you will end up will *"manageable"* children.

The nurses, my mama, nobody told me during any one of the times I laid in the hospital beds that my precious and beautiful babies would eventually turn to their own selves. Those little whimpers turned into roars. The peace I had known could turn into stress in an instant. I must have missed the mommy class that told me from that moment on my life as I knew it would change; denying myself rest or even showers were just the beginning. My money was not my own; it was being held hostage by diaper packs and baby formula. Things did get easier with each new baby. Thank you, Jesus for THAT! Experience is one of the best life teachers! These tiny humans depended on me to be everything they needed, wanted and more. The expectations of being a mom were real: protecting them, not letting them fall; holding them just right; even handing them over to people who adored them, praying those hands and kisses from others were not full of germs. Making sure they were bathed and groomed perfectly, saying the right words at the right time. With my first baby I became overwhelmed fast! All the determination and all the things I said I would do and wouldn't do, was now somewhere under something that made it not visible, so it was left unattended and not visible to me, mentally in this moment. I still wanted these things, but the weight of the demanding responsibility of a new child was now in the forefront and blinding me from any plan for this big bright future that was so graciously planned out for her. Emotionally and physically; there were too many changes all at once. I couldn't be who I was *(or who I thought I wanted to be)* and keep up with both the demands of another helpless person and the demands of life. Before I knew it, I slipped into postpartum depression. I mean it was like a blink of an eye; it was as if it happened between changing her diaper. At one moment I felt completely fine. Then, as if a light switched off, I was sad, unhappy… *depressed. What was I supposed to do with these feelings?* I tried to hide them for so long; still laughing at the right moments, calling who I was supposed to when I was supposed to, just to say, "Hey Girl," showing up where I needed to be, smiling when I was supposed to so on the outside everyone seen this parent who was happy and doing so well with her new baby…but deep down I was so sad. I was now this person who I didn't recognize. Negative thoughts of bad experiences and pain started to consume me. Yeah, "Pain," was overtaking me and with a vengeance, determined to put a strangle-hold on my very existence. How did he get back into my life, and better yet where was everyone who said they loved me? I became very lonely. Little by little I begin to isolate myself. I went out less, talked to friends less and just wanted to be alone. I completely fell in this black hole, a place of no return. I decided I was no longer needed, no longer wanted; *so why live?*

As I lay in the hospital bed, tears streaming down my face, soaking the white hospital pillowcase. Staring up at the light in the ceiling, that seemed to flicker every 25 seconds… I remembered it all:

The pills.

A letter of desperation I left behind.

The final phone call.

The ride in the ambulance.

But here I laid, I was still alive, but what I wanted to know was how did I get here? I mean HERE, in this moment of my life, in THIS situation? *This mentally dark place.*

They are here! Now what?

That day I laid in that hospital bed I remembered, just my daughter father at the time, whispered to me, that my daughter needed me. It was like something switched in me instantly! I knew this, I knew she was given to me for a reason. His reminder hit me so hard. It was as if God had sent an Angel to speak directly to my spirit. Those words *"She needs you"* translated to *"Get up and live!"* That tiny whisper but yet there was so much power in those words, that gave me *Life, Purpose, a reason to Live.* I went from *"how did I get in this place,"* to *"Im going to do all in my power to be the best mom I could be!"*

If someone would have told me as a teenager that I would end up with three kids, I would have called them a liar! Having three kids and balancing each child's needs is no easy task.

But I can't imagine my life without them. Their very existence has changed my life for the better. When I became a mom at 19, I had no clue what I was doing. I had to grow to be intentionally involved with my children though. I started off learning and providing the basics. Food, shelter, clothing. Then to potty training, walking, reading, writing. Then to principals that weren't learned at school like gratitude, respect, prayer, ethics & more. Then teaching about society, relationships, money management, life-time learning and more. Each time I mastered one thing, I was eager to find another way to be more involved and teach them more. I became more involved as well by volunteering at the school, in the classroom, to be team mom of a sport, I wanted to be involved and I wanted them to feel my presence in their life. This was a feeling that I didn't get in my childhood. I devote a lot of my time and energy into making sure they are successful, now and when they are older. I begin to create strategies and principals for them to live by. One of the principals I have taught is always remaining active. They say, whoever, *they,* is, that an idle mind is a devil's playground. This is true for children as well. My children are required to be involved in 3 activities. They are required to be involved in serving at church in some capacity, they are required to join a group or club from school and they are required to be involved some way in the community. This allows them to keep God at the foundation, learn to interact with social groups as they grow up to be productive citizens of society, as well as help them learn how to give back to their community and those around them. This also allows for them to form relationships and creates positive social circles for them to be a part of with those who share their same interest. Its healthy to be around others who share the same interest and can motivate them. This does however create a lot of responsibility with juggling their activities. Balancing my schedule and their schedule is not always easy. But anything you want, you find a way to do it. I have created a schedule system for our family that works. A weekly schedule is visible so that everyone in the house knows what's going on and when, they all are aware of the expectations for each week. I had to put myself on a schedule as well. That includes personal scheduling, setting alarms, set days for chores and shopping, meal planning and so much more! See the key was knowing what I wanted to do, not giving an excuse as to why I could not do it but finding a strategy that will help me accomplish what I desired.

I make sure my children were exposed to things to help them think outside the box that society tries to put them in. One of the most important things for me was that they are life -long learners. Learners beyond the classroom of schools. Learners who started at home, went to school and continued learning even after. Putting in the time and work necessary to make sure they are successful. See as young African Americans, society is already set up against my kids. For my son, a young black man in America, society wanted to ruin his chances of being successful the moment he was born. As a mother I knew I couldn't expect my children to get everything they needed from school. I needed to include lessons and conversations they wouldn't get from a classroom; and I needed to be intentional about doing it. You see, being intentional takes being involved to a different level. It's making sure I listen to their desires, their thoughts, their needs and helping them by guiding them on the right path with wisdom, with love, lessons and responsibilities that will help them be the best *"them"* at any age. For the most part I know the paths my children will take based on their desires, talents and gifts. As a mother it's up to me to see that they make it down that path of success. And what is success? It doesn't mean millions of dollars or fame, or anything else society has as the idea of success. It's being the best you that you can be; no matter where you are in your life. That's what I want for them always. To always be grateful for where they are but to always strive for more.

It wasn't until I really discovered my *"Purpose"* and my role as a mother in their lives before this became clear. See for so long I thought I was just here to:

Nurture.

Protect.

Raise.

Release.

Nope that's not all that is required of me as a mother. I have to be involved in their day-to-day lives, to teach, to provide wisdom, to provide an open door, to make sure they have access to the best resources. *Guess what? You don't have to go beyond your means to give your kids the best either.* Been there done that! There was a time in my life where I was foolish and purchased everything, everything they whined for, every activity I seen for kids, I felt like my kids had to have or be involved, only for them to play with the "toy of the moment" for what seemed liked

20 minutes then lose interest. Or get to the activity and decide they really wanted to learn how to skate and not take ballet lessons. This does make you a mom who wants to give her children the best! This does not make you intentionally involved, whether you can afford it or not. For me this became old, real fast! Lots of money down the drain, trying to please their every need, feeling guilty for things and trying to feel better by *"buying things."* I change had to happen and it needed to come soon! I needed to use wisdom when it came to raising my children. As a mother my job is to create substance in their lives. Nothing that's here one minute and gone the next. What experiences can I create that will teach them something or provide them a life lesson. Responsibilities to earn things, working hard to accomplish goals. Staying with something to the end because you made a commitment. Yes, they are still kids; they need to have fun too but the lesson of, working hard, earning things, accomplishing goals and being

true to your word are values that I need them to learn and always have.

One day, a really long time from now, when I pass away, I want my children to see how I was a wife, mother and a business owner. I want them to respect and value what I do and know that one day they can do it too. My girls don't have to choose between being a house-wife and having a business. My son doesn't have to choose between being a Boss and having time for his family. Each person's healthy balance to life is different, but there is one that exists for everyone! I am still not a perfect mom. I still have challenges and run into new obstacles all the time. I still get overwhelmed, I still get angry or disappointed. Just like my kids are learning, I am learning on this mom journey too! I have just made up in my mind that I will be intentional about helping them achieve the success they desire. *Why?* Because they are so worth it!

PRENEUR

Entrepreneur-One who organizes, manages, and assumes the risk of a business or enterprise.

Merriam-Webster definition

Entrepreneur- A person who uses their gifts and talents to produce a cash flow. Someone who is extremely bold, probably does not have kids or established their business way before ever having kids. Someone who does not otherwise do well on a 9-5 job. –

A.K.A a "preneur."

Tramika's definition

What really happened…

I Came Out

After getting married and with children, being a housewife forever was NEVER on my radar! I started working when I was 15 and I decided I liked the money! Not only did I like the money, but I loved the competition of trying to be the best in every position I held. I'm secretly competitive! I could see myself now - a position in upper management, making tons of money, giving my kids anything they wanted, and living a lavish life with my husband. You see, I loved the early morning hustle and bustle, the highway commute, blazers, pencil skirts, stilettos, Blackberry devices and French vanilla coffee. I was living the life; or so I thought! Year after year of working in Corporate America brought me so much joy. I was a hard worker and the harder you worked, the easier it was to reach the top. I was a BOSS in Corporate America. You couldn't tell me anything! Learning came easy to me. I was easy to train and caught on quickly. Getting the job and being promoted became a game to me. I would clock how quickly I could reach the top and how much money I could make doing it. And the bonuses that came with it. Oh my, did I love those! I would work on jobs and after a 6-month period I would be promoted. Then 6 more months to year after my first promotion, I would be promoted again or moved to another department for something different to do. To be honest I would get bored with my positions, quickly! I would master my job in about 4 months, then I would be ready to move on to the next assignment.

When I relocated to Georgia, my whole life changed. It was no longer hard work paid off; it was a new game! What mattered now was who you knew and who you were willing to get to know to move up in the company. This was not my game, nor did I know how to play well. I remember I kept saying to myself, my work should speak for itself! See, I was a self-sufficient and hard-working woman who worked well alone. I didn't need to be connected to or know certain people to move up. *"I can do bad all by myself,"* was my thought! Well, working for this new company in Georgia turned from bad to worse quickly. I hated that at this company, it was all about who you know, and I hated the situation my kids were in. Although I loved my job, I loved my family more. I wanted to always be there for my children, the job was second to family, as it should be.

When we moved to Georgia our children had to do after-school care for the first time and it saddened me. They already did 6 hours at school. They needed to be home to rest and relax for the next day, not on to the next group of people who essentially were co-parenting with us. By the time they were picked up and home for the evening it was bath time, with dinner and bedtime shortly after. This made me so sad. My children were with strangers more than they were with me, *but who really was the stranger in this case?* It got worse as I was denied time off for field trips and holiday luncheons, award ceremonies and classroom presentations. Sitting at a computer saddened by the fact that my child was always being disappointed - looking at every parent walk in the door with anticipation, hoping it was me and then being hurt by the fact it would be *"Jimmy's"* and *"Sally's"* mom. I felt as though I was letting them down. I tried to suppress the feelings with, *"it's the new millennium, everyone does it! There are a lot of working parents."* But that only lasted for so long. I began to hurt more and more. Sitting at the computer, not working because I was sad and mad that I couldn't just do what I wanted to do turned into being in AUX and trips to the restroom to shed tears. I got to a point where I couldn't take it anymore. I needed to be there for my children. This challenged everything in me! I was in an uncomfortable place. *Do I step out on faith and leave all this money Lord? What about bills and the needs of my children?* Then I began to think, after taxes and everything else, was it really a lot of money and was ANY sum of money worth me missing out on cherished moments I could never get back? These were all questions that had me battling thoughts in my mind. What was the right thing to do? After much prayer I was reminded about the gifts and talents that were placed inside of me. I was reminded that I had a loving Husband who would support me. I was reminded that I had children who needed me. Most importantly I was reminded that *"His Grace is Sufficient!"* I wasn't valued in Corporate America and would be replaced as soon as I left. Every day I stayed in Corporate America, trying to "climb the ladder" and work to make "CEO Bob" rich, was another day of my dreams being delayed and a waste of my gifts and talents that God had put inside of me. I had a certain level of value there. But there was a place where I was needed! First, for my family and for the group of people who were waiting for what was inside of me! Well, I'm happy to say they no longer have to wait! *I CAME OUT!* I came out of the myth that

Corporate America was the only way to go, the only way to make money to provide for my family. I came out of the myth that it's every family's American dream to *"climb the ladder"* in someone else's company. I stepped out on Faith! I'm now my own Boss and my family is now reaping the benefits. I have never been happier!

Let's go back to how I came out…

It ended over swim lessons

I never had an ideal company that I just had to work for after being laid off from my *"dream job."* I applied with whatever Company that was hiring and paid the most with the best hours at the time. I knew how to ace the critical thinking and personality test; and it always led to an interview. An interview was all I needed to get my foot in the door. I knew exactly what to research before my interview always doing my homework. I was confident - a beast when it came to interviews! By far the best interview I had was for a company that was the end of my corporate career. I walked in the interview like a BOSS. Not that I was cocky, I was just very confident in my interviewing skills. Now I will be honest, this interview was a little different. I was interviewing with way more people than I ever had; there were four of them. They asked the typical interview questions and I gave them the same answers that I had used for years. Not made up stuff, real stuff that had *actually* happened. This one was a little different. I could always tell by something they said or a look they made that would let me know that, yeah! I got this! But not this time. No facial expressions from anyone. Everyone wore straight faces and spoke in monotone voices, asking the questions and writing down my answers. No slip ups of them saying, "Yes, when can you start." Has that ever happened to you before? To Me? Yes, lots of times I would get that verbal nod. Not this time, though. To clinch this interview, I knew I had to pull out my secret weapon. I had rehearsed the company's mission statement and spit it out to them like it was a motto that I had lived by my whole life! Yup! I *"kilt"* that interview and sure enough I got the job! We relocated from North Carolina to Georgia with this job and my husband's current job, and within months I hated it! I had never felt this way before. I had usually worked for pretty good companies, did my work, went above and beyond, got what I wanted from my supervisors, climbed the ladder and got raises as I went along. Yep, I was that girl! You know, the perfect example of leadership on every team, the type of employee the boss wished he or she had more of. I followed all the rules to a "T." When you told me my job description, I did it precisely! This job started out like all the others before that one. I would settle into my new job for a bit, do some research on the next step, and eventually go for it. I would get that promotion or department change; but something about this job was different. I started the job with training of course. It was so boring, week upon week of what felt like never-ending training. I was eager to get on the floor, have my own desk and my own area, and to be great in my own space. When that day finally came, I started off with a great supervisor. He was a Christian man who was very understanding whenever my kids were sick, and I had to call in. Not only was he really understanding and kind about my circumstances, he was a great leader for our team. He kept the atmosphere family oriented on our team with celebrations of birthdays, potlucks, etc. He was a really kind guy. I met and connected with a lot of people on this team, it was by far the best part of the job, the people I worked with. One day my supervisor wife became very ill and in a blink of an eye, this kind supervisor that had me holding on to the job was removed from the picture. My supervisor position was moved to another department that was not so demanding, where he could tend to his wife a little more and our whole team was split up. We were all divided up on new teams. Everything for me at this company went downhill from here. The new Supervisor I now had was a supervisor from hell. A *"brotha"* no less. He was so busy trying to appease upper management for selfish reasons that he forgot to be a leader first. The numbers of our team were a clear indication of that, we had very low quotes out of the entire company. After trying to escape the Supervisor from hell by applying for many jobs in the company, it became very clear that I was on that team to stay. Company policy was that my current supervisor had to recommend me for a different position. Since my numbers held our entire team up, he was surely not signing off for me to go anywhere! Upset wasn't the word. One day the company posted a perfect position, or so I thought. I could stay with the company long-term, maybe even retire from the company. It was an event planning position, totally up my alley, totally my "Moe Joe," totally my thing! I had applied with high hopes, just to be declined. The feedback I was given was, "not enough experience." What?! Did ya'll not see the number of years I had planned personal and community events? Soon after, another position came up with the same department with just a promotion of responsibilities and money. Of course, I applied. By now I was really bored. I needed something new to do and more money. It was time! Do you think I got it? You guessed right! Nope, denied again. The feedback was that I should go shadow someone in that department to get more experience. Soon I came to realize your hard work in this company, shoot in this state, does not speak louder than who you know. Who you know will open doors of opportunities and like I mentioned it was a new game that I was so unfamiliar with. This made me rethink everything. My perspective changed completely towards work and towards Corporate America. Was I ever really winning? I went from applying for other jobs to just completely being miserable at this job. It was as if the blinders I had on just came off. I started feeling as if I was being seen as nothing more than a number. Nothing more than just a front-line employee to get the job done; never really being valued. I started looking at my personal life and how I wasn't there for my kids when they had classroom parties, school luncheons, awards day, field trips, etc. I had put this all in the back of my mind while working full time because the bills needed to be paid but anything they wanted that I could buy, they had it. We went on trips, dined out, they had everything right? I really started to question a lot of things. *Are they missing me? Am I missing something? Do they need more from me? Is this job really worth it?* After feeling this way for a few months and sharing with my husband how I felt, I knew we were in no position for me to quit until I found something better. I settled into being miserable, angry and unproductive while working for this company. I did bare minimum work day-in and day-out. I decided I wouldn't apply for any promotions, I just wanted out! It was then that I started applying for work-at-home positions. After all, I had to work. That was a part of being the help- meet. I needed to "help meet" the amount of money that was needed to sustain our household! I begin to cry before going to work, cry while on calls, in between calls, rushing to the restroom before anyone could see me and wiping my eyes until they hurt trying to stop the flow of tears. I wanted no one in my business. *Don't ask me no questions. I ain't telling you nothing!* I looked into counseling; maybe it was me; maybe I was tripping. The American dream is to earn a decent living, do a job close to bearable to financially support your family to the best of your ability, right? What happened to the old school days of the wife stays home and tends to the home and the kids, while the husband goes out and works. The husband brings home the bacon and the wife fry's it up. That was out dated for this generation, right? After all we were millennials! *What household didn't have two working parents? That was the new American dream… right?* A great career while being a loving wife and great mother. But I was missing something. I felt it in the pit of my stomach every time I cried. I prayed and prayed to God to open an opportunity for a work at home job. I could still make money and be there; or at least in the home with my children. These were questions I repeatedly asked myself day in and day out. This work from home job was sure to be a blessing for everyone! I could be in the home when the kids to come straight home after school, I could cook dinner on lunch and have it ready for my man! It soon seemed like the dream life! Well after sorting through the companies that paid like $.02 an hour and the companies that weren't necessarily legit, I found a few work-from-home companies and applied. All said I was overqualified. This just turned into hurt, pain, bitterness. I now felt like I wasn't doing myself justice or being a great mom for our children. *They needed me!* They needed me to be more active in what they were doing. I had run out of ideas. I didn't know what to do but to cry, pray and cry more.

We had just relocated to a new city and I remember seeing an email about free swim lessons and thinking yes, I'll sign my daughter up for this. The only problem was I needed to get off work at least 30 minutes early to make sure she was there on time. Vacation time. Yes, I had vacation time. I would just use it every day for 30 minutes to be on time. I submitted my request to my supervisor *(you know the "brotha")* and I was denied. Denied? *What?!* He had kids. Didn't he understand the need to be there for them, even if it was simple swim lessons? Little did I know that deep down inside it was really bigger than the swim lessons. How dare he deny me something

I worked for? So, I submitted another request: take 30-minute lunches and use the other 30 minutes of my lunch at the end of the day. Surely this would work. This would be my sacrifice and compromise for just a week. Denied again. I was furious! I was upset about the denial, angry at my supervisor because it was something he could make happen. I was frustrated because I couldn't do what I wanted to do, and I felt sad, as if I let my daughter down. Yes, I know - *all over swimming lessons!* And she had no idea of the lessons, I hadn't even mentioned them to her yet. I immediately started to cry. I was messed up for the rest of my shift. I literally might as well have clocked out and gone home because I was not productive for the day at all. Immediately, I started praying and asking God why I was here. I already knew the answer; I needed the money. I had other questions: Why was I so unhappy? Why did I feel like I wasn't a good mom? Why did I feel as if I was working for a dead-end company that I hated? *I just wanted to be free!* Then I started challenging myself to think about how I could make money to contribute to my household so I could quit this miserable job and be available for my kids. *The thoughts of this felt amazing!* I had honestly never thought of myself doing anything but working in Corporate America. The feeling was rejuvenating to say the least! It was like a side of my brain that I had never tapped in to before. I begin to ask myself what I was good at. Of course, event planning came up first. That would take time, marketing, lots of hard work. Not that I wasn't willing to put in the work, but I needed immediate, consistent income. Babysitting! It might sound elementary, but as a mother, I knew that every parent needed a good babysitter! Ok so it sounds a little more grown up… child care! The thought came up and settled in my spirit with such a peace. I could take care of kids to supplement my income. After all, for about the last year or so, I had watched my co-worker's kids while they went on date nights and took mini vacations, and I did this all for free. I could go into full time babysitting. *How much would I charge? How*

many kids would I keep? How would I make this
work in my home? Who would I tell about this?
The thoughts, questions and research became
so liberating. I told my husband about the idea
and we both agreed that it was time, time for me
to make an exit and be there for our children, be
there for our family, attend to our household first.
In 3 weeks I would take the biggest leap of faith,
probably the biggest leap of my life! Leaving
Corporate America… Becoming an Entrepreneur
was no easy task. It is not for the faint at heart! I
am still learning daily, finding my way in this
world of entrepreneurship. I am most proud that I
did it for me, and not only am I happy for me, I'm
happy for all of those around me who seen my
leap of faith and see my journey as I grow,
especially my children.

Finally, Wifemompreneur…

WIFEMOMRENEUR

WifeMomPreneur- A multi-tasking Woman who can balance being a Loving Wife, a Nurturing Mother and Run a Business as an Entrepreneur.

Tramika's definition

So here I am, ready for the next phase in my life! What an incredible journey it was to get to Wifemompreneur. There were many days when I couldn't see the other side! Days when I wanted to give up, cuss, yell, walk away and never look back! Days where I felt like I would never be the wife my husband needed, days when I felt like I was a bad mom, days when I felt I could never wake up and not punch a clock. Days when I felt like how could I possibly balance life and its many responsibilities, balance the HATS I wore…and still have time for me, still find my place in this world? There were days when I felt I needed to appear as if I had it all together. I didn't, and it was torturing me on the inside. Days of stress, being overwhelmed, dealing with fatigue, silent frustrations and more because I was trying to be perfect! What kept me is My Why, My Purpose; Who I was called to be and ordered to do. I had to discover the purpose for our marriage and that keeps me married, there is something bigger then the two of us. I had to discover the purpose for me being the mother to the children I was sent by God, that keeps me from not giving up even when I have repeated myself a thousand times. I had to discover my purpose for Tramika and who I was meant to be in this world, that keeps me going even when I feel discouraged. I learned a lot on my journey to Wife-Mom-Preneur.

In each phase of my journey I was so afraid. What pushed me was a bigger strength; I have always been determined to get the results that I desired, no matter what.

I am becoming the complete woman I desire to be. The wife my husband needs, the mother my children need, and an entrepreneur who satisfies a need I see in so many in my community.

Most of all, I am becoming the woman God needs me to be. I believe we all are on endless journeys until our day of rest.

So, I will continue to learn, continue to nurture, continue to teach other wives, moms and entrepreneurs.

I want to be a great wife, mother and role model to other women, as well as do something that completely, whole-heartedly makes Tramika happy! I want to be great in every area of my life! Yes, it takes more time. Yes, it takes more sacrifice. Yes, it's more to handle. Yes, it's more to balance. But this is my desire, so I had to find a way to make it happen.

I learned on my journey, it's not about being the trophy wife, a super mom, a perfect person! Matter of fact, perfection isn't even necessary… is it even possible? What do you desire your life to look like? Now go for it! I had to come up with a strategic plan that works for me and my family so that I can create what I desired.

I am so happy to tell you that at the end of it all, it's worth it because it brings me joy! I am so happy that I have finally found my place in this world, my why, my purpose. Continuously learning, I can confidently say that at each stage, I strive to be Great in every area of my life!

I pray this book has been an encouragement to your life. I found out that there is no perfect time to get your life in balance and under control. Here is what I say to you:

- **Start right where you are, with what you have, and doing what you know how to do.**

- **Paint the perfect picture for the area in your life that you desire to move to the next place of success in and build a strategic plan to get you there.**

- **Remember to have patience; but be consistent on the journey.**

If this seems like a lot all at once, it will be just that. Remember, always take one step at a time.

When you shift your mindset and become intentional about what you want your life to look like, including saying yes to You! That's where the first place of transformation happens.

My Love Letters

I would like to thank God for the strength, the insight and the wisdom to become an Author. It was not an easy journey, *at all!* I am grateful to God that I was able to not only start this project but finish it and there is more to come!

To my children, thank you for your patience and great behavior. Thank you for doing what was expected, it gave me the time to do what was needed to push this baby, "book" out! Thank you Kaniya, Samai and Terrell Jr. I pray that one day you can inspire the world with what's inside of you! By speaking, writing, by any means necessary! We all have a story to share! Becoming an Author was just one stop on my journey, I am grateful that you all get to ride this ride with me and I pray it motivates and encourages you to create and take charge of your own journey!

To my Family and Friends who encouraged me along the way, THANK YOU! For the times I said I couldn't do it, for the times, I put it down and you asked what that status on your book and it forced me to pick it right back up. For the laughs we shared during the process. For randomly answering questions *early mornings* and for telling me I could do it! YOU WERE RIGHT! Thank you!

To my editor, You ARE THE BOMB!!!! Nothing less! Thank you for believing in me! Thank you for riding the journey with me, although it lasted longer than I wanted. You were understanding and gave it to me how I needed it. Thank you! To my readers, thank you for purchasing my book! Thank you for seeing something in my journey that has inspired you to read more, I pray that you are Empowered to live your BEST Life Ever!

Last but surely not least! I could write a full book about your LOVE and SUPPORT! To my Husband, Terrell Sr. You have always been patient with me. Not only with writing this book but since we met. You took a chance on this broken Girl and I thank you! You have always seen something special in me, even when I didn't see it in myself. You have ALWAYS put me first and supported anything I wanted to do. For that I am grateful! Thank you for your many sacrifices, both seen and unseen. You have had my back through it all! You are the Dopest person I know! I am so happy to be married to you! Not only my journey but Our journey has been nothing short of AMAZING and I am so excited for what's to come! Thank you for being my coach when I needed you to, and when I didn't need you to, lol. You encouraged me and you pushed me. I have never loved a person on this earth more than I love you! I am Forever Yours! ... By the way! You are next!

About the Author

If I can do it, you can too! I am now a "Wife-Mom-Preneur," A multi-tasking woman who can balance being a Loving Wife, nurturing Mother & and run a business as an Entrepreneur. I have my own company, Prestigious Events by Tramika Craddock as an Event Planner & Event Consultant, I am a Success Strategist to the "Wife-Mom-Preneur" where I help Women live balanced & organized lives through strategic planning, I work in Ministry, I am the Founder of SHEnetworks, designed for women to work, win and celebrate together. I volunteer for several organizations, and so much more! I now have my own identity, I gave birth to what was inside of me, my own dreams and desires that I have for MY life, My Purpose! And because I am true to myself it helps that much more in all the other "HATS" that I wear … So now if someone says, "His wife," or "Her mom" I say, "whoever she is, She is Dope! I call her Tramika Craddock, Wife-Mom-Preneur!"

Most important is that we remain true to ourselves, our identity, our own dreams and desires. It's important that our identity, dreams and desires don't get lost under one of the other "HATS." If you haven't already it's time to give birth!

Booking Info

Email: TramikaCraddock@gmail.com

Website:

TramikaCraddock.com